# OUISCONSIN:
## THE DEAD IN OUR CLOUDS

Bryan Tomasovich

*Julie / Steve...*
*Neighbors...*
*Cleaner than the Beatles*
*White Album, but so*
*deeper.*

**Emergency Press**
New York

*2005*

Printed in the United States of America

Published by Emergency Press
531 W. 25th St.
New York, NY  10001
emergencypress.org

Emergency Press is the imprint of the Emergency Collective.
A New York non-profit organization, the press is also a member and grant
recipient of The Council of Literary Magazines and Presses, and a participant
in the Green Press Initiative.

An on-line study guide, or 'primer', meant to complement
*Ouisconsin: The Dead in Our Clouds* is available
on the Emergency Press web site.

ISBN 0-9753623-0-5

9 8 7 6 5 4 3 2 1
First Printing

Cover painting by Gregory Klassen

Author portrait by André Pretorius

Grateful acknowledgment is made to *Coelacanth, DIAGRAM, the Emergency Almanac, 5 Trope, ISLE, Jubilat, Milwaukee Orbit, Massachusetts Review,* and *Nimrod,* where some of these poems first appeared.

"Clouds Empty Light" was awarded second place in the *Baltimore Review* annual poetry contest, 2004.

*Ouisconsin: The Dead in Our Clouds,* by Bryan Tomasovich, won the 2003 Emergency Press book contest. The author would like to thank Lorna Belkin, Michael Belkin, Aaron Belz, Jason Gitlin, Christopher Grimes, Jayson Iwen, Gregory Klassen, Ander Monson, André Pretorius, Scott Zieher, and Henry Williams for helping to make possible the publication of his first book.

Dedicated to

my great-grandparents
Krist and Katarína Tomasovich

and

Amanda, my wife...
the truest home for this immigrant

Jarrah and Arnica Bee


and for stories, databases, and advice contributed
to the serious stuff of poetry...thanks to

my family, immediate and extended

the Anderson's of Fall Creek, Wisc.

Peter Szenasy, my Slovak teacher

Anton Treuer

United States of America Immigration and Naturalization Service


James Liddy, John Goulet, Sheila Roberts, Peter Sands, John Koethe

C.K. Williams

Christopher Grimes, Jayson Iwen, Scott Zieher, Nick Flynn, Jason Gitlin,
Molly McQuade, and Ander Monson


and in memory of


Frank Tomasovich, Sr., Peter Tomasovich, and William Matthews

# OUISCONSIN:
## THE DEAD IN OUR CLOUDS

Nimbus

Cumulus

Altostratus

Cirrus

"I do not know if you will like my poetry or not—that is, how far your own inventive persistence excludes less independent or youthful attempts to perfect, renew, transfigure, and make contemporarily real an old style of lyric machinery, which I use to record the struggle with imagination of the clouds, with which I have been concerned."

Allen Ginsberg to William Carlos Williams in *Paterson*, Book IV.

"The orthography of Indian names has not, in every instance, been well adjusted by American authors. Many of these names still retain the French orthography, found in the writings of the first discoverers or travellers; but the practice of writing such words in the French manner ought to be discountenanced. How does an unlettered American know the pronunciation of the names, Ouisconsin or Ouabasche, in this French dress?...Our citizens ought not to be perplexed with an orthography to which they are strangers... Where popular practice has softened and abridged words of this kind, the change has been made in conformity to the genius of our language, which is accommodated to a civilized people...The true pronunciation of the name of a place, is that which prevails in and near the place."

Noah Webster in *American Spelling Book*. 1831.

"Wees-kon-san...was the Chippewa Indian name for the Wisconsin River, meaning "gathering of waters"...The French voyageur called it *Ouisconsin*, the first syllable of which comes nearer to the sound of the Indian than does 'Wis.' An attempt was made, a few years since, to restore the second syllable of this name to its original Indian sound by substituting *k* for *c*...the attempt, however, was unpopular and the Legislature solemnly decreed that the name should be spelled Wisconsin; and this, probably, more from opposition to the individual who attempted the restoration, than from correct literary taste, or any regard for the original Indian name."

James S. Ritchie in *Wisconsin and its resources; with lake Superior, its commerce and navigation. Including a trip up the Mississippi, and a canoe voyage on the St. Croix and Brule rivers to lake Superior. To which are appended, the constitution of the state.* 1858.

NIMBUS

# MILWAUKEE ROAD

Milwaukee is connected to Chicago and St. Paul.
The name of the railroad tells us so.

The big man on the tracks, lying
in his stocking feet could be a stranger, then.
His socks, however, are worn at the balls of his feet
by brown leather, as are every man's.

I approach the big man from the direction of his feet. They are upturned, heels
rooted into the ground. His pants legs are torn at the seams and his belt
is ripped from its notches.

The man's chest, no matter how large
would not hide his face. Not at this distance, if his head was intact.
Here is candor, then. This man will never know where his shoes flew to.

His hair and brain tangle in one another,
one a dam, one a glue. The blood

cannot soak into the inadequate scalp and the bloodied hair, saturated as it is
will not be made equal to the wind. A decapitated head is a nest

a living turbine curled up one last time, and turns into nothing
but patches on the railroad ties.

But I am the interpreter here. When I mention the blood, the picture
becomes far too calm. So I go back to the shoes, at his sides.

I mean to tell where I spent a minute
of my life, when it joined anxiously
with a mechanized suicide. A planned wreck. A path and a lost head.

There was none of my saliva in anything I tasted: instead, the shale dust
upset yet in the circumference of the body's site
the hot leather smell of thrown shoes
and the outburst of a body that is done feeling down to the bones.

What I taste is need for more people
to take this man away...this wreck on purpose.

I carry a heavy hardbound book

and it reminds me that this man and I, we need company.
Before that, we had just death and life, suicide and life, and at the center I rock
on my toes and heels, gaining and losing that sparse distance.
I go pale and flush, and staring
at this stranger, this is a difficult luxury.

I am tired of the direction I took to meet with a mangling such as this.
I am tired of holding the book.  It is extremely compact, so much so
I know it first as pure weight, an anchor
but then the strain of holding it
brings me back to the emergency. The book is my only reminder
that I cannot take care of this man, this extraordinary accident, this mess.

Because, in the book Odysseus rests
for a moment when a man is freshly killed.
Then, he moves on because he is in medias res.

If we witness
Odysseus grieve, that means we are not him.

                              Big man,

I once rode the knees of other big men...
my grandpa, my dad, my brothers.
I straddled the backs of them, too, until my feet touched the ground.
Now, I am not a kid, and men I do not pretend are horses.
I'll say that before the end I wanted a horse
to be shot out from under me...
a spectacular sacrifice of horse, dying without a scream
same as the Indian rider, joined finally, living up to one brave death.

But now I'll not touch this invitation, this man's body
once so perfect for a kid to ride.

Start at the man's feet. They seem to be two levers that released his bowels
and thinned his head to a mirage gone down the tracks, challenging me.

Now, with Odysseus on the Milwaukee Road
go back to the shoes.
The force that jolted through this man
and kicked off his shoes, I live in the middle of that.

I started life in the middle of
                    such an emergency.

4

# OUR DEAD IN THE CLOUDS


The dead are clouds and the dead bring rain
while we work all the hours the gods made...

the dead, makers of rain falling on our days
we cross out on calendars. Rain gurgles
white ripping down hills, fills the river
and our palms, runs between beaks and teeth.

Rain slips down serrated and smooth vines
and leaves moss on the fences, gathers
in troughs hoed up. It is fertile as we allow.
Whistles the old-time seductive flute of prophesy
and romance, completes the octave in all of us.

Rain falls from the dead on our knowledge
of the weather, falls on traditions of forest
prowess, even the brimstone of our city.
And we know the weather in our bones
and the sound of gulls chanting and chewing
amongst our rain, falling from these clouds...

some fine shreds of vertebrae found only in the sky.

It is rain that falls when we look into the grave
with the only phrase we can muster.
And it is rain that reminds us for a life-time
what we said.

The falcons we breed lift from one skyscraper
and through the clouds make their boldest dives.
The crow finds its black gasping progeny
in the fog. The ant runneth with ash. And we
survive the burnt wool smell of rain. Dead are clouds

and our melisma, our passage sung on one syllable
our stories leading us in and out of conversation.
Rain falls from weather we know like destiny
washed from wind made from hollow bone of the cosmos

mixes with the sacrifice of warm milk breaths
of children and rote memorization of the old.

The rain melts you or me or anything in between.

Fell when we could still talk amongst the animals
it falls in the wind that makes the body flail
and cringe. Rain adheres skin
when we lose our outlines of limbs in the storm.

Prehensile, the rain falls from clouds wherein
are the dead, grasps the bat's song and the worm's
sticky path, falls on hoarders and spendthrifts.

On makers, the cheap rhetors and old geezers retired
from breweries and tractor factories
all the same.

Rain falls on the deepest boss voice in town
on engineers streaking hands through balding hair
entrepreneurs bragging about seven generations.

Clouds are the massive motion of our convection. Power
and resistance moleculing for days and years. The weather
depends on the way we turn our cheek. And in the same sky

clouds are our "oops-a-daisy," our murderous teasings
of each other's immigrant names, our love ballads depicting
a woman's thin wrist, our vespers, and bloodletting.

Clouds are at crisis height. Not neutral, but charged
with our civil pride or perversion.

So when the dead bring rain we are often surprised
that our freaked, fecund home
can wear and tear so well.

# SON OF TOMAŠ

I step into the bus and her face I know
is cut out of familiar sky

        could be a cousin

her eyes dark, not round
but the start of square carpentry
of the jaw, the forehead

her Old Country mouth.

        This lost Slovak cousin

she will not speak to me
not even in Milwaukee

in earshot of the noise early this century
cramped in back rooms
of Ludwig's tavern where the great-grandfolks
first made up home in America.

Such a new country I remember it all.

I go back to the kid in my ear
to cooing of recipes
too vulgar to keep, back to cussing, rising
from the guts that practice perfects

        and I was weaned from that Slovak
        a little American

so I recite this cousin's words in the bus, a quiet test
of the durability of my mouth
to bring home our language
but when I make the Slovak sounds, how nervous...
even novice by now, are the habits of my face.

How hypnotic her beauty. It is more an old folktale
and works this charm for she is crystal
within ore of my grandfather

his intricate fame

        for speaking the last Slovak I knew.


These few days past his death I have half felt
my face think with his character,
with these Slovak features. Now I feel my bones
are crushed in these crowds
for the way I miss him.

        For missing my own face
sleeping in mixed blood.

I should go now and put my ear to her mouth
in the middle of this old
washed-up city in America.

        I swear
all my life I've wanted a foreign wife.
Needed to regain the physique of those immigrants
that became my backwards ancestors.

To bring home the syllables
located in my name, Tomasovich:

        son of Tomaš.

Grandpa, he never wrote a book
but saved coffee and tobacco cans instead.
Collected nuts and bolts, seeds
and coupons on the farm up north

sorted out the miscellaneous
with me, knee-high
my blue undisciplined eyes and curly hair
of a Polish prince. For him

        I concocted my Slovak wife.

*But a man gets all slicked up, and goes into town*
*only to find the first girl who owns*
*a pair of sturdy legs*

*and thick blood, or else*

*no other favors come farming this Godforsaken land.*

Say that in Slovak, Grandpa:  Godforsaken land.
But don't say it'll get me nowhere.

# WOULD NOT TRADE MILWAUKEE FOR THE REST OF THE WORLD

Coming home, I
trade for moccasins
buried in tamarack marshes

and villages of wild rice. Trade for moraine
trade for fresh water, cold bowl of lake water
drinking the spring ice crashing.

Leap shore to rock to ice block
to swelling berg
to forest of winter storms on horizon.

Trade for cold bees lying with sapped out leaves
trade for fruit that is a pair of seeds
the hot tea of Indian talking through the trees
last spirit of fear
fear warning the hot bag of breath in the snow.
Trade for once ample land and the gusts that remain
so that alone
we do not rule our own songs.

Trade for those old days of my own in this town
by which I spoke of love. Now
I cannot instruct the way to count love.

I return for the freaks
and wintry clouds that will affect my dreams.

I live for the freaks
supposing I've severed a hand and count my friends
on what is left.

I said the opposite on the plane, I know.

All the friends involved
in homecoming...how long after I looked away
from our town? And yet an acute many of those spasms are lasting

like the leaping-touch of those tamaracks.

But who cuts his nails, and who wears them down?

What sadness I trade
for madness and normalcy of these freaks

in my story told on the road into town...

Languages of tribes I miss could say this
but they are down and out:

*there remain only pages and pages more*

so the immigrants:

restano foglietti
il reste feuilles encore
es bleiben noch blatt ubrig
nu nog velleties
marad me lap
ostaiu listica

or: a ešte zostava vela stran...
in the Slovak.

# BUMBLEBEES AND BUTTERFLIES


These freaks aware of the bumblebee's failure
are in fact bumblebees. What they learn
by day they tell us
the same dull day. They bungle publicly, and chase
the mean disaster
of sirens.

Butterflies are the long-lasting bruise, rhythm
over city river, whimsy atop the museum.
Sun burns a black spot
in their eyes, these butterflies
but rarely do they get picked out of the sky.
They are our magic by day, and opprobrium
at the curfew bell...

disorderly opposite to the bumblebees.

Perpendicular streams...
the old moment and the young moment, these freaks

two padded hammers playing out
a different, but primordial ceremony of flight...
concentrated here in Milwaukee like no other town.

Some argue memoranda and others create
plainsong, an isolate hum.
Their combined rhythm
does not reveal
*miscellaneous* whatsoever in our town.

Freaks of low unemployment, freaks handing out newspapers
freaks who love the smell of brewery yeast...

See, their song is a long tongue of lumps,
song behind the autumn trees
and song on a wire. Song on two wires...

curdling, illegally camped at the river

song of police undercover

songs of the bosses, tit for tat tongues of subordinates
"clever-town" songs.

Our town is freaks.

Freaks hover
the mobius strip
of Germanic streets
and old socialist meeting halls.

Freaks hold our town tight at the corners
they fly at eye height...this
bumblebee
and butterfly crisis height.

The town has no chance to be bested
by a circus.

# CLOUDS EMPTY LIGHT

Face it, a good many of our dead return
in the distance clouds travel in a year...
the cycle of a cloud-year, not mock belonging
to the land, like my believing
I've come home to stay.

I groan under hard work
that makes me lucky, while the billowing dead

hurry to the Lake, pedal, burst, and conflate.
I do not think the clouds will empty to earth
all their light before I leave this town again.
My homecoming...

the opposite of hypocondria?

                              I lean
against the old brewery and the light surrounds me
not from the sun, but clouds. My brazen
brain is related to the old grandfolks
who once lived up the street.

Now evening
denies the clean shelter of human sense.

Rising clouds and sunset umbrage, how they filter
the light, and where is the glint but ribbons
of old trolley tracks embedded in the road?

On the old brewery hill once the streetcar
bent the corner around.

The dead in clouds...or spiders in cobwebs?

An alleycat yawns and his mouth is a picture
of our hearts. Touch him where he's not mangy
and hear the inflated leap of a "snake dance."

Light from clouds, anabiosis that rinses
the angry chores from the river, it frees
me so I can ask what it does foretell.

Steam shovels haul poison silt
locked to the dam by generations of papermaking.
The dam is deconstructed now

and in the future the river will rectify
the spillway, the burble gurgle river replace
hurdy gurdy dam.

Constantly (under clouds today) the river is
redirected and the rain loosens
its most symmetrical hard work while

a lone fisherman
casts and cranks his crazy songs to the catfish.

Each monster pulled from the water he calls
the daddy, the mommy, the baby...and when the torque
of his cheap aluminum rod exceeds certainty
the metal snaps
and gouges his hand.
This fish is "granddaddy."

The lone fisherman speaks a lot of new immigrant
language then, pets the cat I followed
to the river. He strokes the fur with a bloody hand.

"Always something aching," he explains the cat to me
in English while he feeds
the namesake guts to him.

A glint of garbage rises from the offal of the river
fish. The dead constantly empty light to earth.

Oh in what vernacular, and what
                          to explain next?

CLOUDS: LAST WILL


Building beaver effigy mounds
I practice where I find no roots...

the beach

and I dig and sift, sort weed and alewives.

My beaver I carve

I learn old Potawatomis ways
my fingernails go
back in time.

Tail lifts off the cloud-cockoo land
and bears toward the Lake. I start early

while I am fresh, the snout of my effigy
veers east. Minding
his own business

my beaver.

            Say I am blond-eyed.
Say I should see more pride
in shipwrecks.

But I am a madman who has the strength for it
and could I unshadow my dead
I'd prop them in my beaver.

Practicing mounds high off
the half-moon beach
where skipping stones reincarnate.
Where Solomon Juneau says Indians raced ponies

where he called them 'warriors.'

Where the horizon laps backwards when I stand atop my beaver.

            Up the tributaries
my olds, the first wave

dead in their homesteader's peace.

Much bickering
and trading since, over remaining cemetery plots.

Except the young uncle, for him an eternal flame.

If not for the cleansing and burial
clothes he'd smell yet
of his good collie.

Let me not go absent a dog, and be lonely for barking
the night I go to my outrageous grave.

               Building for the long-haired, long-toed
curious girl, too

she kissed me once a week through summers.

Last time I saw her I was looking
for the leaving road

the town had just broke
1000 and was celebrating that.

She waved to me from the parade
flute in hand, marching
in place. Then other wind instruments, silver

and some black, narrowed to slip through the cemetery gate.

       Practicing a beaver
who minds his own business

based on Increase Lapham's diagrams for the Smithsonian

and accounts of the pioneer farmer
pointing to the moraine
where he'd finished the plowing.

Schlitz and Pabst breweries
basement excavations, too.

Boots gone to rot when I started keeping
to myself upstream the dams.

Practicing in sand

if I'd run a backhoe all my life
then dig me a grave near the freeway, I'd expect it.
Cobwebs are meant for such men.

But handspade's the way
to a proud moment. Dig
and tug ten little
front and backhoes I muster

and palms the size of a beaver.

Beavers
spread-eagle gulls
suckers, even practicing
the calm ugliness of suckers.

When I go I'll volunteer
my wind pipe.

You chop it up for bait.
Catch a dozen more like me.

I've room for my remains, estimated
by height of this beaver:

the horizon

seen from height (h)

is at a distance
roughly equal to $\sqrt{2Rh}$

where R is the Earth's radius...

Leap up with a phrase
to visit me.

Stand on my beaver, my oversoul.

Look out...
gain the sight of an extra half mile of clouds
on the horizon.

I, the undersigned...

CUMULUS

## WHAT SURVIVES?

The walk from the Menomonee Valley
to 5th and Walnut, kitty-corner
the Schlitz Brewery, and

the handbill survives, stashed in Kristian's suit pocket
urging him
forward to America, war brewing
in the Balkans.

English is funny:

war is brewed
and this beer is brewed, one free drink he'll find
in his brother Ludwig's tavern

after work. Things look up.
Kristian is listed in the new city directory
for the first time since they arrived.

Louie corrects him: *Things are looking up.*
No more dirt poor, cooking the neighbor's soup bones
making whisker tea
being so hungry, could eat the ass
and chase the rider.

Not long ago, Kristian was standing in line
at International Harvester.
He was a farmer once
and they manufacture farm implements.

Made sense.

Harvester gives you a handbook with the job.
Learn English and they help you gain citizenship.
Keep your nose clean, they'll hang
your photo in the cafeteria framed
by tiny stars and stripes.

Who is this Paul Schryer? The Harvester boss
making a speech so the hiring line
was at a stand still:

*If there is one man in this organization who would hesitate*
*to alleviate or less the suffering of the men at the front*
*I would advise him to go somewhere out on the prairie*
*away from the gaze of civilization, and drain*
*the yellow blood out of his heart.*

Kristian landed a job when Harvester
shamed a few Germans and Hungarians
out of the factory.

But he's changing his mind in favor of the railroad
while his wife cuts his hair. He explains it three times
to Katerína, things so damn complicated
in America. The handbill

caused them trouble from the get-go. Sent it
to the Sokolovics, her relatives immigrated years ago
to New York. To translate the details.
They say it's a game of roulette but nonetheless
it is a big country:

> *300 men needed for railroad work in Wisconsin*
> *and other reaches of the northwest. Highest wages*
> *paid. Free fare. Ship tonight. C.W. St John's Agency.*

Offers come from the Chicago Milwaukee & St. Paul Railroad
were not the common crock of shit
Kristian had run up against, now that news
was the Bohemian Jews, first in line to snap up the jobs

with most the townsfolk eager to ship them out
to settle railroad land up north
in the boonies next door to the Indians...
they can't buy the jobs now. All's gone awry

since the foreman knows Jews are inept at tilling the soil
from reading he'd done of Tolstoy novels.

See, I got ears. That's why I panic.

An immigrant is a stranger
who *starts* with a bad track record.

On the other hand a man works hard, builds boxcars a few years
in Milwaukee, stays out of fights
shows up sober
turns a deaf ear on union agitators
changes his clothes and bathes

yep, yep, throws all else in
and swallows the American First patriotic garb
the company'll naturally put trust in him,
set him up with a homestead plot.

Just to secure their holdings, populating new lines bought up
from the defunct Weyerhaeuser Railroad.
Weyerhaeuser still holds the monopoly on lumber
so when Chicago Milwaukee & St. Paul buy up Weyerhaeuser
they're needed yet for cutting ties and building bridges.

Goes way back to Weyerhaeuser buying up the Chippewa Falls Line
cheap, run by those Pound brothers
Thaddeus and Ezra, shut down
when they printed their own money
and all sorts of general usury.

It is complicated Katarína, but see?

The railroad handbill is three years old—ancient
compared to progress made by wheelers
and dealers from Milwaukee, Chicago, up and down
the Lake all the way to Detroit.

Downstairs, in the bar Louie was talking to two Slovaks
out from Detroit. Used to work at Ford, these two,
and the way they tell it the bosses ask Poles and Italians
to volunteer
teaching English to employees off the boat.
Learn English, name the presidents, and so on
and so on and they hand you a certificate, help you
get citizenship....but on the way, what pageantry:

the brand new citizens enter a stage dressed in clothes worn
in the Old Country. If you threw yours out
Ford keeps a supply for the purpose
to convert you. So center-stage
in borrowed clothes, you undress and jump in to American
street clothes and progress in a line off stage.

This goes on in the cafeteria during lunch.

Pow. Just like that I'm an American
and no more dirty-cuss immigrant.

...Who was Kristian Tomasovich?

Maybe
he ripped off this tirade
in Slovak.

I know he talked only when he needed to

so maybe he stood at the window
combed his cut hair
quietly and accepted the America
America was

while Katerína cooed to his sons
learning English as she went along.

Rubbed his mustache and dreamed
of the homestead tucked way up on railroad land
between the Chippewa and Thornapple Rivers.

Maybe Kristian stuck his nose in his new handbook
for more English.

*I hear the whistle. I must hurry.*

*I change my clothes and get ready to work.*

*I work until the whistle blows to quit.*

*No benefits will be paid if you are hurt or get sick
as a result of having been drinking.*

But the Slovaks do not mix their tenses
and this last one, too hard tonight.

Some have proper grammar, and others
eat what is left.

Outdoors even sweethearts are volunteering
all away for a worn-out try at English:

> No more drink.  No more fight.
> For cryin' in the night
> let's go to bed.

# TRAIN SONGS

Iron stalagmites were tempered in fire that destroyed the derelict
Chicago Milwaukee & St. Paul Railroad works

a re-enactment of forges from the heyday

boxcar and caboose hitches
and wheels, pignoses
of ancient engines

melted to iron stalagmites. Say eyewitnesses

fellows who ran hoses
even bulldozers and wrecking balls, knocking down
brick walls to suffocate the fire.

But burn she did the night through.

Moths thought extinct joined the firelight
and gulls, even swallows chasing their sweetmeats
fell difficultly into the heat, when

                              pyrocumulus

seeded by thermals supernatural
towered above the rush of common smoke

formed its characteristic nimbus anvil
and doused the factory fire

with a phenomenal roll of its belly
teats unloosed

and the cool of cloudburst
so abruptly changed the temperature
that wrought iron melting
was suspended in mid-air.

This train-lava froze in descent
etched into knife-edged roots
instataneous and eerie.

Cinders hissed steam and all was lost:
terra nullius.

A great collection of dead in the clouds leaped to that pyrocumulus
some first-rate rail laborers panicked
but assembled in the sky.

They say a picture of the works on fire
capped by the inferno cloud
is worth a thousand words...

but what words? The Chicago Milwaukee & St. Paul
already derelict at the onset of the fire.

All had lost the languages of their old country long before, all farmers
became the company of immigrants
who flooded into Milwaukee
to prove they were *100 per cent American.*

A thousand words...

Depends on which words...English words, those romantic
hillbilly train songs about an engine built for speed?

My stories, cut off from the Slovak, are shy
of being a century old. But begin in the hot
handiwork of boxcars and cabooses.

# PANORAMA REVIVAL

The entire press and pulpit of Chicago endorsed the new panorama

the biggest of attractions, Karl Frosch's
Jerusalem on the Day of Crucifixion

and the opinions of distinguished clergymen
were front-page stuff:

Rev. C.W. Leffingwell: "A grand theme, grandly treated, and destined
        to become a powerful help in the promulgation of Christianity."

Sold out all its shows in Milwaukee and was tugged
on barge to Hog Town, to the corner of Wabash and Panorama Place.

The Crucifixion
350 circular feet long and 50 high

*a picture without boundaries*

      *a contrivance, an apparatus encapsulates the rotunda crowd*

*a novelty of perspective*

a view of nature that after 150 years of experimenting would turn
a soul inside out.

Experiments with a spiral staircase to disorient
the viewer on entry.
*Spherements* with light via the rotunda roof dome...
silk screens (before war-time parachutes, mind you)
shredded hessian, and smoked, ground
and glued glass.

At 628 W. Wells, Milwaukee, the light in the studio
shined from the Crucifixion by means of reflection.

*La Nature a Coup d'Oeil*
the Irishman, Barker, had coined it when he made
the patent application
from his dimly lit jail cell.

Rev. Dr. H.W. Thomas: "Frosch's Crucifixion arouses my interest, and I feel
that its influence is decidedly for good."

Who is this Frosch? Lured along with panoramicists
from Berlin, Dresden, Weimar
and Frankfurt... "enjoy German theatre
German newspapers
German beer gardens. We affectionately
call it, Little Munich."

Frosch leaves München for the Milwaukee Panorama Studio
to work in the style
of mass-production. Outlined the Crucifixion
on a grid system based on Frosch's sketches
done in the Holy Land (although some say it was Frederick Heine
the man from Leipzig
who had studied in Palestine).

Each man knew his part for the Crucifixion
pushed around the studio on scaffolding
pulleying up paint, pushing it around the canvas.

August Lohr painted the halo and clouds, anything in need
of chiaroscuro. Franz Rohrbeck, Roman guards
and blood on the ground. George Peter handled
the crown of thorns, the cross
and a few shanties in the background.

Heine, once a foreman in charge of the production
of The Battle of Atlanta
covered hair, sheep, all metal.

A few second-generation boys who stood out
at the newly formed künst academy
were put to the task of molding and stuffing 3-D objects
to hang from the roof. This, the faux-terrain, blended
with the bi-dimensional canvas. Mostly the apostles.

The few mistakes Frosch made he dabbed with a silk necktie.
He painted the wounds of Jesus.

And Christ's head slumped on His right shoulder.
This detail of the panorama
shows Jesus tenderly biting

into his own shoulder
the deep knot of muscle there
loosening in sacrifice.

A wound, both bruise
and a flowering of concentration
that would come to a martyr while staring down
the last frustration...familiar enough

stuff Frosch could witness at any popular
turnverein
when a man over-exercised his gymnastics...

but divine too. The last contact with flesh
and from this detail of Jesus, the entire panorama crowd
would evolve. A reflection
on loss, some spiritual accuracy in Hog Town.
The criterion was to meet the sob
offered by Jesus, his last chance
at mobility. Be sure this was a moving grimace
and no thin-lipped smile.

Rev. Hugh Latimer:  "Grand! Sublime! I wish we had more pictures like them,
     the world would be all the better then."

Then...Frosch's Crucifixion was dismantled and removed from Chicago
by court order.

The world had more pictures like the Crucifixion. This one a hoax,
plagiarized.  Exhibited 3 years earlier
by Frosch's old boss in Goethestrasse, city of München.
A boss
with a boss's name: Bruno Piglhein.
And he sues under new U.S. copyright laws and wins.

Milwaukee in a rut since the panorama revival died
when something bigger
and more electric than Little Munich
was set off out west in Hollywood.

Why not, if no *original* fervor for Jesus exists
amongst the old Milwaukee panoramicists, look

to our own backyard? Did we want religion?
Marquette blessing the savage Indians.

Battle scenes? Black Hawk and Tecumseh.
The frontier was ample and no small-time.

# FARMERS SET FOOT IN OUR TOWN

Makers set foot in our town ready to plant
in a fertile kingdom; immigrants bartering, trading
ready for the bending moment, hands to the soil...

the undulating manna movement
of new fields and strange rains from gold clouds.

Came with heirloom seeds
exchanged by grandfolks
great nobles and peasantry alike
prizing their seeds more than currency.

Seeds sewn in the mother tongue
became an American harvest:

Juicy tomato...the Bitchyeh Gertzeh
turned to Bull's Heart;
a variety grown for bragging purposes
to separate men from the boys.

Druzba picked from the vine as 'Friendship'.

Black Sea Man, Tomato Stream, Hungarian Heart...
a whole new tongue of Eponymy.

Not the plastic ears, the waxed bells, and groomed mandrakes
trucked to superstore aisles
a thousand miles plus...

but the Diamond Eggplant bred for flavor
and Forellenschluss: lettuce speckled like a trout.

Moon and Stars Watermelon
Small Shining Light. Ah, seeds to spit
bitten from twisted, oblong fruits.

Worth standing in line for.

And flowers to plant: Glittering Prizes,
Night-Scented Tobacco, Out-House Hollyhock,
Salpiglossis.

All pollinated by new variations of bees
and butterflies and bats, new rain, a lime count
not the immigrants' own, banking on a strange angle of the sun
in the cornplanter's kingdom.

Nothing the same
but aroma and fetid muskiness of Lemon Queen
and Velvet Queen Sunflowers, and dreamy waiting
for Kiss Me Over the Garden Gate to climb the wall.

Set foot in our town with seeds
but not even their own dung heap.

Not aiming to starve, what with Cucumber Parade
Bull's Blood Beet
Georgescu Chocolate Pepper

and Slava z Enkhuizen ideal for sauerkraut
until the Lusitania sank
and to prove patriot...Liberty Cabbage was coined.

Ready to plant in clouds of pollen
blown from shaggy cathedrals of pines, ready
while others loafed in observance of Independence Day.

Ready to farm with a hessian bag full of seeds
and a few Blue Marker potato eyes.

Hunkering down for longevity.

To pass down the farm.

# CZECHS AND SLOVAKS FACE THE CLOUDS


Maxídiwiac, or Buffalo Bird Woman, for two summers took on an academic boarder...far away from WWI. She taught the young man, Gilbert Wilson, ways of tending Indian corn and beans. Buffalo Bird Woman's son acted as interpreter. She was old then, and knew little English, but went on collecting blue ribbons at the white man's county fairs.

Wilson and her son sketched seeds, planting pouches, field layouts, and garden tools made of bone and odd metal leftovers. Came to call each other 'brother' by the end of the second summer when Wilson returned to the university to present his master's thesis in anthropology.

Never did become a manual, this thesis

for Kristian and Katarína, who were eager for instructions
to help carry out their dreams on the homestead.

These old Czech and Slovak folks, family and neighbors, sought
the New World...
came in dark ships, boarded in cramped neighborhoods
and worked in factories. Money-saving years in hand
they hurried by train to the northern pinelands to discover a farm.

Believed they landed the genesis of pride.

Instead, they would expose themselves to the clouds, irrevocably...

Kristian and Katarína found only the dark again
in the woods. They stood in the understory
of the pines, their vision curtailed..no horizon, and little sky.

A few machines and plenty muscle cleared a place for a farm.
But no part of the Yankee instructions for homesteaders
revealed how to withstand the abrupt contact
with the dead in clouds
over a strange land, and how to survive what the clouds offered:

history
of the original people who met with more than death
by natural cause.

Sell the timber and use the profits to buy farm implements, yes.
But they opened land
in a matter of weeks
to the slow smoke of peace
and corruption mixed for thousands of years in the clouds overhead.

The dead in our clouds over Wisconsin let fall their light
on even our slightest history. Only what the clouds expose
collects in our memories
no two ways about it.

Wilson's mentor was Professor Albert Jenks. Advised Wilson to use more Latin when discussing an Indian woman's menstruation. As a girl, Buffalo Bird Woman used to occupy a watcher's stage in the fields of corn and beans. They planted these vegetables in mounds interspersed, to deter weeds...not straight rows we are accustomed to.

The watcher's stage was constructed out of pine logs and built around a large shade tree standing in the middle of the field. This took some planning...the fields were burned off each fall, expanded here and abandoned there—the boundaries changing.

The stage stood about four feet high, the height the corn would reach by October—when the leaves fell from the large maple or dogwood shade tree. In this way, she and other girls warded off deer, rabbits, birds and even little boys who would steal corn and roast it in the woods.

Several families shared this field. The girls would sing special watcher's stage songs, passed down for generations. One by one, they'd grow into women and be replaced by younger girls.

Once a woman was turned out of a girl, evidenced by her first menstruation, she could no longer sing amongst the corn. Buffalo Bird Woman's people knew the power of fertility within women challenged the spirits who gave life to the corn each spring. The corn spirits would hide and turn the people's affront on its head...rather than dying the spirits saw to it that the greed in those who cared for the fields spread into the life of the corn, and this excess would ripen the corn too soon—the ears sprouting misshapen, freakish smut and disease.

Slow days on the stage, Buffalo Bird Woman sat and made baskets for her father to collect tobacco blossoms. A buffalo's scrotum was filled with sand to stretch and stiffen it. A small strap of hide stitched to the top made a handle. Buffalo Bird Woman said the scrotum of a buffalo is the toughest part of his hide.

Kristian and Katarína knew little *time*
in America. More acres than years.
The task at hand was to *improve* the land, to overwhelm
the place. The homestead manual challenged
that no white man or woman had ever made this place home.

No one had gotten it right this far north in Wisconsin.
Trapping, mining and logging...the dead in clouds overhead
their new home, whites and Indians
already exhausted that progress.

The sense of farming forest land where the few open tracts were swamps
fit for cranberries and rice
amounts to the swift stick of prejudice on the part of Yankees
to evict Eastern Europeans from the cities. If, scattered
up north the immigrants could haul their meager stock of corn
and wheat to the train lines
to help boost the supply to Milwaukee and Chicago, all the better.

For the Czech and Slovak neighbors, the farms meant freedom
and a chance for the dirty underdog to win. If they conceded at all
it was those winters the men returned to Milwaukee
to work in the shoe factories.

Then came the rocks underfoot
and the clouds overhead.

Kristian and Katarína with their neighbors worked together
on adjoining plots, the Liskas, Evicas, Slaseks
and Cibeks...a tight band, not just neighbors but a small colony
reminiscent of collective farms vital to the history
of the Old Country.

Germans and Polish...their faults the Czechs and Slovaks knew well
and steered clear. Advice from Indians disappeared
to the reservations at Lac Court Oreilles, Flambeau, even White Earth.
Chippewa that dissented, the homesteader's manual warned
were dangerous and lazy.

Tomasovich's, Liska's, Evica's...all their children were born
to pick rock...clear a path for plows
in the fields, rock that heaved from the thawing ground each spring

when the web of pine roots were torn out
dynamited, and burned
gone for good. How many generations could love this new place?

And daily, on the farm under clouds, the light was divvied up
out of their favor. Rain was out of balance, mixed
with hail and tornadoes and a sun
often too puny to ward off the early frosts.

A few of Kristian and Katarína's friends stayed, the rest
sold off their parcels and disappeared
into the city again.

Kristian and Katarína knew little *time*
in America.
How much time would pass before the farm would succeed? After all
other Czechs and Slovaks were making a name for themselves.

Aleš Hrdlička landed a job in the U.S. government, head of the Smithsonian
Institute. His decisions appeared in the newspapers. Dr. Hrdlička was a model
immigrant citizen.

Bohemian born, he immigrated with his folks to New York as a boy. His specialty
in the field of *the antiquity of man* was "anthropology of the insane and other
defective classes," says the historian Capek.

Hrdlička and Professor Jenks were commissioned by the Indian Affairs Office
and Department of Justice to establish scientific methods to discern blood
status amongst reservation Indians in Wisconsin and Minnesota...

Who were full-bloods? Who were mixed-bloods—descendants of the metis
people formed through unions with Ojibwa people and French-Canadians—often
partners in the fur trade?

Hrdlička and Jenks acted on the Clapp Rider and the Steenerson Act of 1904 and
1906, shifts in the laws set up to buy Indian lands. Lumbermen and bankers who
doled out mortgages had bargained with Indians for 40 years, already. Mixed-
bloods were taken in hand and persuaded that they should be guaranteed the
same rights as any white man—to sell their land if they wished.

When allotments where first assigned, a 25-year trust period was set up for
all Indian-owned land: they could not sell their land nor were property taxes
assessed. A generation or two could go by to learn the ways of real estate
trading.

25 years is a long time to wait. Lumbermen and farmers pushed the government to introduce a 'competency' clause into established Acts...if Indians were deemed competent to sell their land, then so be it.

Jenks and Hrdlička entered the fracas to help establish who amongst the Indians was competent—namely, whosoever carried white blood in him was intelligent enough to bargain in real estate deals.

They traveled the reservations examining Indian specimens. Two tests became decisive: the Scratch test, and the measure of hair follicles.

A blunt object, usually a fingernail, scratched against an Indian's arm revealed either a pink wound or brown. Those who reacted by turning pink were deemed mixed blood, if too their hair quality revealed a certain measure of a curly nature—for Indians beyond dispute have straight hair.

Jenks and Hrdlička admitted the margin for error in their measurements. They conducted the tests on themselves and during experiments, found that both men were related to the "Negro." Studies of Scandinavians found that the circularity of their hair samples (curly hair emerges with quite a flat stem) made them more Indian according to Hrdlička, than the most Indian of Indians—the southwestern Pima tribe.

The government needed a measuring stick, however, and these two tests stood. The 1920 roll on one reservation, White Earth, tallied up just over 400 full-bloods amongst over 5000 who owned allotments.

The dead in our clouds curse us yet...
their method is to bring Buffalo Bird Woman's secrets
in the cirrus
face-to-face with Hrdlička in the low nimbus
studying the "antiquities of man."

He is not so safe in his office of a-good-example.

What we think are bygones
become the perpetuity of clouds brewing storm
and freakish halos, sundogs
and twisters. And the immigrants who learned what it means
to be *between a rock and hard place*

account for much of the labor, yet...common cumulus.

Should I not recover
Kristian and Katarína's land, let the Indians
in court today win back their ancestors' plots...

Let the cursed light of clouds not spare my memory.

Let these pages be my own watcher's stage...practicing songs
to ward
off stealing.

# SKUNK FRANK EPISODES

*water, its own calendar*


All along
Skunk Frank knew that the Weendigo would steal him
on the Flambeau. Shack and all.

\*\*\*


Skunk Frank's fishing hole on the Flambeau River is marked
by an alert pine draft
when standing in the ruins of the old Indian feller's shack.
*Go make yourselves at home*
our Grandpa Frank'd say...log frame
tin billboard walls, tar paper
tumbled down and mossy
as the river but colder
home-canned jars, melted fork
bottles plenty, granite chimney shards
but not a feather.

Friends like this...our Grandpa Frank is
a real puzzle.

\*\*\*


Rapids-foam charges up at the falls
and coasts in the grain of the eddy
circling and stained by tannin.
Short ways below Big Cedar Falls
backwater swirls counter-current
appealing to granite and pines.
Thus, strong bass at Skunk Frank's.

\*\*\*

*Skunk Frank, sure, he had feathers.*
*But they blowed away.*

\*\*\*


Thicket or cave, described
is far darker. Even throw in
contrast, some fool's gold
in silt. That will not count.

That is plain imagination.
And not Skunk Frank's.

\*\*\*


Skunk Frank was caught by Weendigo
when fishing was still good
before Grandpa Frank even knew us.
Way back before Grandpa's folks
come from the Old Country, Weendigo's
family was starving. He needed medicine
to help him hunt. He asked a chief, and first
day out, medicine in hand, he surprised
a whole village. Changed the people
into beavers. Ate them up. Ate so much
he forgot his family.

\*\*\*


Grandpa Frank'd fetch his thumb a while in the mud
and manure of the Folgers can.
He liked to talk.
And not constantly bait hooks for three cousins.

Job done proper was done once, half dozen worms
on a No. 4 hook made a ball of bait
with lastibility.

\*\*\*

We'd fish our way to a pail of bass. *Largemouth*
*where the mouth extends past the eye.*

Bobbers we watch hide in the foam sometimes
circle and strain and we cry
and complain. Then bobbers disappear, fish on.

\*\*\*


Grandpa Frank'd carry a can of mosquito lotion
the size of a small milk can.
*The old Injun*
*he'd rub bear fat into his chest*
*to shew bugs. When he snagged*
*up and lost hooks I brang him*
*he'd just whittle bones. But pert ner*
*always I give him a few Eagle Claw brand.*
*And I give him a few bottles of Grain Belt.*
*Thought I was the nicest son-of-a-bitch he knew.*
*Met him years ago*
*at the logging camp.  Had a good heart*
*Skunk Frank. Bit of a loafer though.*

\*\*\*


No...bones?
*Sure, brisket of a partridge.*
No...bear fat?
*That or squeeze the juice*
*from the chewing maw of a deer.*
He prayed to thunder?
*I'll be a son-of-a-damn if he didn't mumble*
*to thunder. Goddamn, what was it?*
*Animkee, Animkee. Sounded a bit like Milwaukee.*
*To ward off lightning strikes. Some sort*
*of Injun talk, Chippewa he was.*
*Said thunder was his own grandpa. But warned us*
*of the Weendigo too. Lord, he was some sort*
*of fisherman. Course, fishing*
*in those days was good.*

\*\*\*

Algae gathers on the bull's nose
of a dead pine snake each time
it revolves within the eddy. White belly
length of a grown man
it slides a stiff, rigorous line
through the weeds.


                    Skunk Frank
had not an ounce of bad temper in his bones.

\*\*\*


More Weendigo ate more he grew, a giant
with appetite nothing could satisfy.
Then the villagers he ate
were revived, not as beavers
but as the relatives of a man who
out of revenge killed Weendigo. His ghost
lives on, captures us and makes us slaves.

*Anyone too preoccupied*
*with sleep, playing, or drink. Excess*
*of all kinds. So help your grandma*
*weed the garden.*

\*\*\*


Grandpa was the last man
who used "Injun"
and then only in a Skunk Frank story
then interchangeably
with Indian or Chippewa
or Ojibwa.

\*\*\*


Redhorse carp when on the spawn we'd save
in a separate pail for the mean chickens.
Few fat ones Grandpa'd throw to the bank
in the direction of Skunk Frank's shack.

*Indians smoke carp.*

He'd cut the line, and fling carp over his shoulder
with an old paddle. *Touch them, hell.*
Hooks still in the gullet
carp flop amongst Skunk Frank's belongings.

\*\*\*


We bait up again. *Weendigo, hell he's a bold one.*
Hides in no cold thicket. Such commotion
when Skunk Frank was stolen on the Flambeau
half his shack was blown down, half
disappeared with him.

# FATHER MARQUETTE: FIRST WHITE SOUL IN MILWAUKEE

Milwauski, free the young man
who sent the statue of Father Jacques Pierre Marquette packing
in a leaky canoe down the Milwaukee River

and we promise not to celebrate him as a martyr
or coin a holiday in his name.

Milwauski, he is only a beginner amongst us
in the hobby of genealogy.

He has told the press that you have the wrong man.
Told what a better town we'd be
if instead the statue of Marquette was sent to the salvage yard.
He has said so because he is an aggravated man...

you see, he compares the fame of Marquette
to the obscurity of his own ancestry.

                    Rejoinders and reminders come in
from professors and housewives, lost umpteen cousins
mixed on the Internet,
mail, even f2f (face-to-face)...

Our frustrations:

>Whereas why Christian came to Milwaukee from Bratislava remains
>questionable  except he had a brother who ran a tavern in Milwaukee...this
>brother, Ludwig, his daughters married and took the names of Radobicky (sp?)
>and Hinca, who live somewhere in suburbia Milwaukee. No, for all the
>drinking they did, my lord...no memory of a plum brandy, this 'slivovica.'

We egged him on outside the County Historical Society
on a break from our genealogy.
Milwauski, you know full well the park that borders the Historical Society
is named in honor of Father Marquette.

One of us said: "Wees-kon-san. Get it? *Oui-Consigne.*"

Another actually hissed. "Skip the sublime versions...*grassy place*
or *where the waters meet.* Yes, *Ouisconsin* sounds like the Indian pronunciation
but tell me if it's coincidence that this name is assembled
from words that point directly to buying, selling, and worse.

*47*

The hissing turned into translating...

*Oui-Consigne...*

"Start with *Oui*. Yes. Safe enough.
Now look at *consigne*. A place to make a deposit.
A place to temporarily store your baggage.
In school, it's detention, where you put the trouble-makers.
Throw in something close, *magasin*. That's a store, or warehouse.
Last, that short root, *con*.
We're all adults here...
means anything from useless idiot, to dick-head, to dumb cunt.
At once remarks on the Indians, and French underlings.
All said, a smattering of ruthless jibes
made by rough merchants and ambassadors.
Snidely concealed in what's supposed to be
the proud and pretty name of our homeland."

*Oui*, all right. In short, tempers were sky high.

Marquette moved by canoe, prayed in forts beside compatriot traders...
the coureurs de bois, evasive French phrase
for men who run the woods.

He prayed like a schoolboy with men who turned Indians
into hoodlums to hunt for hides not meals. Men who divvied up the rum.

Then Marquette took the Jesuit cross to the Indians.

And when he blessed the Potawatomis,
Mascouten, Miami, Illinois

he was amongst the first white souls
with a chisel-faced name to recognize
that this territory is a Free Country...
free, no matter the ruin, to do what we choose.

Marquette was honored with a sacrifice

where he camped on the banks
of the Milwaukee River, he and two coureurs de bois
Pierre Porteret and Jacques Largillier
23rd to the 27th of November, 1674.

*Now* we know his coming was so sordid, unnecessary, etc.

one of us said. And Milwauski, *you* know
the root of our state, this Ouisconsin.
None of it surprises *us* anymore

but it properly horrified our young man you jailed.

If Marquette kept the Jesuit oath he did not leave offspring behind
yet he survives...
an icon: the statues, the plagues, the university

and we remain sons and daughters of no-name dirty immigrants

our parkas loaded down with rejections and run-arounds
(it's the dead of winter...remember
you did not find the statue until the ice broke)...

sent from the archives, vital records
the INS, and social security:

>No naturalization papers here they <u>were</u> in Clerk of Court Office but the
>State required them sent to Eau Claire We don't have any of this here all we
>have is marriage, death, birth records for those born in RUSK <u>county</u>.

>Contact the following address which is for the Area Research Center that
>handles Milwaukee County.

>They should be able to tell you if there are Naturalization records for your
>relatives there. Any information on the Milwaukee railroad would be housed
>at the address below. I hope this information proves helpful.

> Milwaukee Urban Archives
> Golda Meir Library
> University of Wisconsin-Milwaukee
> 2311 East Hartford Avenue
> Milwaukee, WI 53201

>Although we do not have any information about them here at the Milwaukee
>Urban Archives, I have a few suggestions for you. First, the Milwaukee County
>Historical Society has the naturalization records for Milwaukee County. You
>can contact them at:

> Milwaukee County Historical Society
> 910 N. Old World Third Street

>I also did a search for records from the Chicago Milwaukee & St. Paul
>Railroad. We have a few books about the railroad company here but I do not
>think they would contain information about your family member. However, I
>did search the catalog of the State Historical Society of Wisconsin and it
>appears that they have the records—including personnel records—of several
>railroads.

>Wisconsin naturalization records can be found in municipal, county, circuit,
>supreme, and United States territorial and district courts. Most
>naturalization records have been transferred from the Wisconsin court
>system to the State Historical Society. Records from various jurisdictions
>have been brought together and are available for research at the Society's
>Area Research Centers.
> Yours,
> the Wisconsin State Historical Society

>I have found that the Historical Society does not have all records. Check
>with the County Court house. Start with a year that you think would work.
>And go from there.

>Note that about 25 percent of aliens never became citizens or made only
>a declaration to become a citizen...because, according to the Wisconsin
>constitution, it was all they needed in order to vote...the alien files a
>declaration of intent (first papers) indicating their intention to become a
>citizen, to renounce all allegiance to any foreign state, and to renounce any
>foreign title or order of nobility.

Marquette's blue blood arrives in the *pays d'en haut:*
land of the north
the highlands, high expectations, a slang form
of heaven...And missionary blood brings confusion.

>What if Milwauski's right, that dumping the statue was desecration? He's
>got historians and theologians who work for the State.

>Milwauski comes from a long line of Marquettes—power is power, even
>though the baton changed from the Bible and cross to a law degree. He can't
>stand for this or his office will turn into a joke. We've nearly lost Pabst. How
>good will he look if Marquette University packs up their Jesuit things and
>cuts out of town?

Marquette, the first in Milwaukee to pray
for every man and woman under his hand
to become a vulture for God.
All is volunteered to him...the languages, the medewewin spirits, furs
and new generations
once born by polygamy.

>Marquette lands in Quebec in 1666, studied Indian language and culture,
>sent in 1668 to Sault Ste. Marie, a mission among the Ottawa Indians, and to
>La Pointe de St. Esprit, meets an old friend, the trader Louis Joliet, at St.
>Ignace on Mackinac Island in December 1672, Joliet has orders for Marquette
>to accompany him on a journey to explore the Mississippi...

>It certainly doesn't hurt to ask the SS Admin to do a search but remember
>that although social security started in 1935 many were not originally
>included in the program. Well into the 50's the self employed did not pay into
>Social Security or have SS #s. This applied to farmers, doctors, ministers, etc.

>Any other 'clues' in the family history that would indicate when the family
>lived, such as working in a certain industry, like logging, or milling, or
>agriculture?

Marquette sees the cedar trees, the *midewatik*
aligned in the medewewin lodge.
He's an opportunist, believes the branches form a crude holy cross,
figures he's got a head start, intervention from God.

To make his case, he ignores the medicine bundles.
Wants to move the Potawatomis from seasonal rituals
to the constant trap of moral sins.

>This is a monumental undertaking and I'm sure the only way they can
>work out the bugs is to have it online. That may be frustrating to anxious
>genealogists but it will be worth the wait.

>Attempts to find material using more traditional resources has proved
>fruitless.

>It looks like they will need a much stronger search engine to keep the info
>available.

>I only get the following: HTTP/1.1 Application restarting. I also tried to
>access this site from another subscription list and I received a "URL not
>found." I'm using Netscape Communicator® 4.-whatever.

>Tried this web site and message said "too busy" then tried later and was told
>I was denied access as I had no user name etc!!!!!

>E-mail me directly if you prefer not to broadcast your possession of this book
>to the entire list.

Marquette is offered a meal and a ceremony begins. He orders
a larger, more coherent crucifix
be built. The Potawatomis sacrifice a dog.

Frustrated amateur genealogists on the wires intra/interstate
and international:

>I didn't find much there, but may be you Americans have better luck. I do,
>however, have in my possession an unopened invitation to something that
>happened in 1968.

>Can someone tell me what county Milwaukee is in? Thank you.

>18:06:49  Milwaukee is located in Milwaukee County, WI

>18:09:56  Milwaukee is in Milwaukee County, WI

>18:10:44  Milwaukee, Milwaukee Co Wi

>18:19:27  Here's a site that helps with the question, What county is xxx in?

Marquette is received as a kind of manitou, or *manidowek...*
a great spirit.

He will not eat until the dog sacrifice made to honor him is removed.
They smoke. At first the Potawatomis trust his sacred powers.
After all, before Marquette
Father Allouez used the cross at Green Bay
to bring sturgeon back to the streams.
Marquette keeps the pipe, calls it by the French name, calumet.

>I have not been able to find my name anywhere.  Could it have been
>Amercanized to something else?  If so what?

>I don't want to cause pain to any family who is still surviving, so I was hoping
>to learn about this independently.

>She doesn't know much family history, says she was always afraid to ask much.

They smoke and Marquette introduces the baptismal
the path to the gate of God.
As an exchange he asks about a passage to the Mississippi, something
he promised Joliet. He renames the Mississippi
the *Riviere de la Conception* months before he sets eyes on its mud.

>(Was this Milwaukee back then?)

>Is there such a town? I did not find it on my map.

>There was a town like that near here...all that's left of it is a bridge and a
>cemetery.

>Is it possible the cemetery was covered by the Milw. River when the dam was
>built?

Marquette is a sober man. He writes in his diary, transcribed later
in the formal record of the Jesuit Relations, that the dual French policy
of trade and salvation are in conflict.

                                        He makes sharp attacks on polygamy
with the coureurs de bois in mind...they adopt the Indian way, show the villages
that the Frenchman's wealth enables him to run with a few girls at a time.
A rogue Frenchman can support many women
in his hunting party. Better than any chief.
It is a free country, after all.

Nevertheless Marquette knows full well
that the *coureurs de bois* follow on his heels
and with a mere sign of the cross, bless the beaver traps.
Young Indian men protected by the cross venture farther for furs
but are murdered by the Iroquois pushed westward by colonists...
or starve in winter. Or come down
with the smallpox.

        A shortage of men leaves the Indians relying on polygamy.

Marquette persuades the girls that God cannot accept the savage
custom of whoring. Marquette's own celibacy is a curiosity.

Marquette's next step is to induct the girls into the cult of the Virgin Mary.

>In case you ever wondered why a large number of your ancestors disappeared
>during a certain period in history, this might help. Epidemics have always had
>a great influence on people—and thus influencing, as well, the genealogists
>trying to trace them. Many cases of people disappearing from records can be
>traced to dying during an epidemic or moving away from the infected area.

>The great-great-grandmother could have died on this trip.  She happens to
>be my disappearing relative.

Savages for Marquette

are not people with houses unlike his own
or foods, tools, and dreams. But people who deny a Frenchman
the grace of simple order.
Of an aristocracy. Of authority. Of the *marché de pelage,* the fur market.

>If any of this sounds familiar, PLEASE contact me. This has been my brick wall.

>PLEASE, I need help finding siblings/parents/grandparents etc.

>If we can pull together as a team and really mobilize the volunteer resources
>in the community, we can provide free access to all material.

>My only ancestral tie before I jumped on this list-serv was the old ditty:
>"My name is Jan Jensen/I live in Wisconsin..."

>You know what I daydream about? How easy it would be to find my
>ancestors if I came from a famous brewery or tannery family. Also, the
>founding fathers too that you mention—Juneau, Kilbourn, Dodge, and the
>like. Increase Lapham, the archeologist. And now Marquette. Come to think
>of it, I've never met descendants of those families in the archives or on-line.

Milwauski, some of us have proper families and others
must eat what is left. You and me, in our old neighborhood...
we paddled down the creek after heavy rains
and pretended to be Marquette and Joliet.

We grabbed cattails, turned them into Indians
and dunked them in the current all the time calling out odd bits
of our catechism to complete those baptisms.  Milwauski,

the crawdads, bloodsuckers, and mudpuppies were real.
Not your new-found plan to hang a sandwich board on our young man's neck
to shame him as a 'desecrator.' That is punishment
easy as baptizing your brother, who was slower than cattails.

>The statue is really little. I've always wondered if he really was that small, or
>if the statue is just not to scale...

One of the last days for our young man at the Historical Society
the trade of his ancestors riled him.
They were tucked away in turn-of-the-century city directories
listed only as Laborers
and if he could only find their trade he'd know why they chose Wisconsin
and, thus, why generations later he calls it home.

Have you seen a man literally pull out his hair
when he realizes how easy it is to be a Blatz in this town?
Thanks to great grand-daddy Val, listed as Brew Master.

>What's funny about Marquette Univ. is they took heat for their Warriors
>mascot and changed the name a few years ago. I mean, who would think to
>combine Marquette with Warriors in the first place? He came here to make
>them all good Catholics, not warriors.

>While you're at it maybe they should have went the whole hog and took
>"Marquette" out of the university's name.

Milwauski, you learned your way from an old line of well-bred brothers
who beat up on one another. Called your sister *putain* for the sake
of the baptizing game.

>About your children trying to find their Indian ancestry, I'm thinking of
>those posts a couple weeks ago about Marquette Univ., and if you are near
>Milwaukee maybe you should try there? I know one has to be 1/8 Indian
>before it's legal.

The papers call our man an "outcast."
All he's done is snapped at a crucial moment in his genealogy, and swore
that he'd sink Marquette
in the river like so much stinkbait
cast to a carp.

>This statue episode deserves little more than a misdemeanor. The
>first step is to jump on Milwauski.gov and inundate the e-mail.

>Stealing a statue might be a bit rash but we got to take what we know to the
>press, etc. AND remember this whole Marquette affair when we register our URL.

Milwauski free this young man.

Or let me warn you...you'll get more than you bargained for:

You pick on that young man, Milwauski
you pick on his whole family.

# BRYNDZOVÉ HALUŠKY

*for great-grandma Katarína*

Suroviny:

| | | |
|---|---|---|
| 750 g zemiakov | | potatoes |
| 400 g bryndze | sheep's cheese | |
| 100 g údenej slaniny | | smoked bacon |
| 1 vajce | egg | |
| 150 g hladkej múky | | fine pastry flour |
| 150 g hrubej múky | whole grain flour | |
| soľ | | salt |

Postup:

**Potatoes** očistíme, umyjeme a nastrúhame.

Pridáme hrubú múku, **egg, salt** a nakoniec hladkú múku.

Vypracujeme hrubšie **DOUGH** tak, aby sa oddeľovalo od misy.

Z **dough** nahádžeme do **big pot boiling water** halušky, povaríme ich a dierkovanou vareškou povyberáme.

**Cut bacon** na **small pieces** a rozškvaríme.

**Place** halušky **in large bowl, add** bryndzu, **and a little bit of bacon fat. Mix.**

**Separate onto plates, top with bacon, and SERVE.**

_____

Anglický

kitchen   oven   apron   eat   pounds   drink   ounces

deer   venison   pig   pork                    sausage

girl   woman   wife   mama   mother country

butcher  castrate  pluck

telephone  truck  tractor          radio  price

farm  go to town  supper                    <u>krv</u>  blood

ALTOSTRATUS

# DURING THE FIRST DEATH

How my brother got it in his head to console Grandma
I don't know. Maybe an accident
placed him next to her while we waited out the funeral.
Even so, this was the moment
when his stiff upper lip would stick.

Young as I was, I was jealous that all eyes
watched those seats up front where Grandma sobbed
more than any wife or siblings
combined. My brother was in that spot
picking up attention

better than Vietnam
on TV where we saw how women
for a few seconds grieved for boys.

Then a tangling of arms happened
sped by a grief I could not figure.

Grandma was not the consoling kind.
No way did I picture her giving up
that harsh posture that steadied her wits for the daily chores.
She was too stubborn for arms
to hold her. We stood in the end to view
Pete's body. The tangling of arms, Grandma's

around my brother turned into a clutch that I feared
was not so lucky anymore.
                              I'll not say that men
in the family had to pull her away from the casket.
But she did collapse over her son's body for a time long enough
to sob, sob so she could come to her senses
on her own, senses that she expected would endure

for the rest of her sad, bitter life.

                              And my brother
all the while withstood Grandma's breaking down
squashed between her and that last embrace of Pete's body.

Finally at the wake someone by the booze table explained
that poor Timmy was simply dragged in with her.

My brother staggered...this same kid who taught me
to stay on my toes
when chasing a pop-fly so to keep my eye steady on the ball
a ball game pragmatic
running like an index finger on a calculator...

he came up out of that coffin
I remember...with a nice, awkward epiphany.

# YARN UNRAVELING

I was born between the assassinations
of Martin Luther King and Bobby Kennedy.

They were shot just two months apart...April 4th and June 5th.

Born at a time in America when there was a lot of grieving.
Who will deny the spectacular in that?

That my crowd picked up on an immense amount of grief,
distrust, disgust, a feeling that we were not safe,
that we were being...picked off.  Picked up

on that as babies, just in our blankets, maybe still in the hospital
being fed at the TV, mom watching the news and televised funerals
of Bobby Kennedy and Martin Luther King...they were huge.

Not to mention Vietnam...all coupled, there was just a lot of lying
going on to cover it up, and no one was soothed.
And let me tell you something, if it wasn't anger or remorse

about the loss of these men, what we heard right from birth was people
saying, "Good for them, cut down to size," or even...
"Someone finally popped the nigger."

***


I was a weakling
the first years of my life

in and out of hospitals
baby teeth stained
by medicines.

Never explained to me
this lepsy I had
to this day.

***

So, yarn...
the sight of yarn unraveling bothers me so.

Uncle Pete was a young man when he died. He was holding on
to the farm, working hard before the brain tumor
forced him into the hospital. Never got to know him well

but I think of him as super-kind, that day seated with my father
watching my baseball unwind.

I threw the ball straight to the clouds, the leather
coming unstitched.
Threw it underhand, up to the afternoon and back
to my bare hands.
Red yarn spooled off the ball, arched
and fell, a trace of fuel
from a rocket. Yarn looped over my head
when I caught the ball.

Pete's mouth was pink with a smile. My aunts had shaved him
and dressed him in brown trousers and a light yellow button-down shirt

and sat him in the sun. Then they went to sit inside while my father talked
to him and tried to bring him around. I was young, and I remember

my father was really young.

I was only cheeks and missing teeth, but at this age I knew my father
was not the reminiscing kind.
Here he sat on his lawnchair, not working on a Sunday for a change.
He expected Pete to concentrate

listening to the stories they knew growing up on the farm.

Pete watched the yarn unwind from the baseball
his head bobbing up and down. His mind was so far gone.

He followed the ball I threw. The ball was faulty but beautiful
and to me seemed a spectacle
worth Pete's attention. My father spoke adamantly to his brother.

Pete was white and fragile from the hospital.
They had let him out to die.

***

And if I went without this memory
I think I'd be more afraid of Pete too.

Pete is a half-understood fear for me
and all the boys in the family. We all grow up expecting to die
before we reach 30.

Now that I'm the age at which Pete died
his memory is...

a certain precipice. And Goddamn it

if there's one thing we need to work out in this country
it's what is hereditary
and what is not.

***

America hypnotized assassins in 1968

to instill the killing urge
and later, to insure their guilt. In-between
the TV had a new factor to report...

the ins and outs of hypnosis.

Dr. Diamond was hired to put Sirhan Sirhan in a spell, and asked the suspect
to describe Bobby Kennedy: "RFK must die, RFK must die
RFK must die," said Sirhan, a parrot.

Diamond supplied the defense with news
that Sirhan was a schizophrenic who hypnotized his other personality
to prepare the murder.

As for the theory of accomplices
the L.A. Blue convinced us Sirhan had fired 10 shots
from a gun that held 8 bullets.

Ran yarn
through bullet holes in door jams and ceiling
to trace the trajectories of shots
in the pantry

of a California hotel kitchen

and made up a new ricochet physics

where a would-be president was picked off...

shot from behind, never mind that Sirhan stood in front
of the Senator.

Meanwhile, every cop in the fold ran us on
a media chase for the woman in the polka dot dress

hoping we'd find a second gun. Guns all of sudden
recovered the guts
we liked about Billy the Kid and his pretty girls.

Anyone worth his salt
knew why RFK was killed. Anyone worth his weight in gold
knew even better:

Howard Hughes
Rockefellers
Shah of Iran
the CIA...

Sweet Jesus, if I was not alive at the time
no way would I swallow it all:

hypnosis
polka dots
and Nixon springing into the privilege
to telephone the men making our first rendezvous with the moon.

Hell, Bobby.
It was Hell when they shot you.

***

Pete's hair was combed straight from his widow's peak
over what had been lost
due to the medicine.

I remember that, too, because our family

used to go to the stock car races
on weekend nights, and my father knew a lot of the drivers.

When I'd have my bath at night, my mom would comb my hair...
5, 6, 7 I was...this was the 70's, and she'd comb it
in a different 'style' each night

in the way I asked, the way one of the race car drivers
would style his hair, the driver

I wanted to be that night.

Then I'd go out to my father at the kitchen table
or the garage and make him guess who I was.

One summer night after Uncle Pete died...

he guessed, he said...

well, just that, "Uncle Pete."

\*\*\*


No, Pete did not race cars.

Just on my father's mind I suppose.

But Dad's guess has strayed on
in my own.

\*\*\*


Dad was not convinced we landed on the moon.

Only fellows dressed in rubber suits
full of helium
grainy TV film
static voices
a crane off camera

hoisting the Eagle in New Mexico somewhere.

Proof? "The surface has a beauty all its own,
it resembles the southwestern desert
of the United States..."
Neil Armstrong, a few seconds after contact.

Simple, ironic play.

We only had to out-do the Russians
he explained to Pete.

Besides, building a rocket to land on the moon
was a chore
Dad could not accomplish
and someone else getting the upperhand, he'd put an end to that
in a hurry.

The sky was still the limit...

the baseball orbited overhead
the red yarn a special
spewing rocket fuel, the capsule and parachute
splashing into my palm.

"One giant leap"
revealed my father's dark side...

People glued to the TV: suckers. Blind
and what's distracting them
is the sight of our own world

in the distance.

***

Ten cousins I knew, locked in the attic to keep out of trouble in summer.

A pair or two of twins, identical twins, among them
looked the same
and I never could keep track of their names.

Some had first names that were others' middle names, and vice versa.

I remember one set of girls was born in May just a day before me.

My aunt had divorced
and bought an old Masonic Lodge
or Elk's Club, or Shriner's Hall...

Four stories, huge open hearth fireplaces, and winding staircases
running through the old servants' cavities of the house.

My mother would take me, spend the day 'visiting'
and send me to play with the kids.

I'd get lost.

Jesus, what she didn't know is
the kids in the attic...

they'd be all hot and sticky from candy, Evil Knievel
and big wheels.

Defecate on each other
stuff plastic toys
into their...orifices.

Vietnam was on TV

locked in with us...
and streakers.

\*\*\*

All along while Uncle Pete was dying, and years after, my father

would go on tirades about mistakes the doctors made
with Pete...

"Fools, fools all them, goddamn fools..."

Blessed be those of us who could be angels, but have the guts
to say Goddamn.

My dad's diagnosis...not, as I thought all along
even as a kid

that it could help cure Pete...

was that when they were back on the farm

Pete one day was hit in the head during chores by a manure spreader.
Knocked him right off his feet
and they had to send him inside the house to take a nap.

After that, Dad says, Pete was always tired.
Hardly make it through milking the cows
without going in for a nap.

We know so little about the bend of our brother's body
as he weeps.

\*\*\*

Ghost, and prisoner

I was not able to fight and strangle you
and that is exactly what you came to say.

You will remain a mystery not to be extinguished
until you identify yourself.

Go ahead, visit me in sleep
if there is no chance better than that paralysis.

How dare you believe I hide anything?

This time, what it took to wake me
were your words meant to indict and repeat
the unaccountable
at the corner of my bed:

*"That really happened to you.*
*That really happened to you. I know it did*
*because it happened to me."*

Pete?

What you should know is that before your visit
I did not breathe
for a long time, through all that I felt happen.

And now I am told you know full well
all
that really happened.

You should know too that in this pipe exchanging all my wind
is a small hole, and that I am screaming
but can let on to no one.

Pete...or are you a quick chemical in my brain?

But when I call you a ghost why is it not a lie?

Come seek more than the outline of me.

I run the water of that afternoon you were let out to die
but the momentum of fear
each young man in our family knows

this you cannot gauge, or know.

I am 30, the age you last saw.

It is happening to me.

Uncle Pete, you tear up the earth of the unearthed past. You stand at the bed
with the smile that unwound when they cut into your brain

and I am paralyzed.

I can hear dogs barking at your name...
at what you would not survive.

# CHRISTMAS DREAM

Pete shares my widow's peak.
Sonny milks cows the same day he marries a girl from town.
The brothers work their muscles the way we do
in the family.

Their tuxedos start clean, rolled up over boots
and bare hands.
They work in that sad chest a family shares.

Sonny's the older brother, married at noon
and the reception to come tonight.
This dream is in between.

I stand in a cobweb room with the milk tank, the cows
to be milked fall way into the distance. I'll dream and
dream. Sonny is my dad after all.

A bottle of watered-down whiskey made to last longer
leans on the first stanchion and I take a sip
to keep the brothers warm and working.

The dream goes on boiled a little happier now.

Pete tries to keep up with his half
of the chores, but he is fairly drunk and under the bags
of the cows he keeps looking at Sonny milking
until finally he says, "Congratulations".

I bet that is all that will be said.

"You'll stay on the farm Sonny?"
Sonny smiles, Pete's his little brother.
He curses too. His virgin is
a few months pregnant.

A flame is pulled against the cold wind
and Sonny inhales extra long.

Sonny, who gets married in a Wisconsin winter?
In November? Got a cigarette, Sonny?

If a wedding has to be, let it be today in a small town
with a pretty name, before an icy winter

dips b'low 0
and embarrasses her more.

All of this is how I dream now that I'm in Wisconsin again.
There was a wedding and I knew the faces so
I followed along. And no one else would dream
these chores.

Christmas night, and I'm on my own. But I've never run from my family.
I constantly love Pete and Sonny.
Sonny is my dad and Pete—he lulls from the dead. He is alone and more
willing to appear than the grief in the family. His name

is not mentioned on Christmas. The dogs barked
on the farm when he died and the dogs still bark at the sound
of his name. Pete calls out to me in this ice country.

He insists on the north of Wisconsin, but Pete does not know
any more about my mother than I do.
He takes me to the milking and his inward leap
of love for Sonny.

The extremes of alcohol will work Sonny harder.
He'll need to finish milking and get Pete
into the cold truck, sober him up for the reception.
The brothers reek of cowshit. No stories
pass that down—I've dreamed before inside the dress
my mother wore.

Sonny will never pay for the wedding pictures...he'll say my mother's lips
were painted too red.

I cannot wake embarrassed and weeping. Pete will be the last
to run the farm. When the family lets the death come
Sonny will surprise us and take a day off work
to manage the auction. He'll say Pete was too young

but not be able to talk the neighbors up
from what bids they do offer, out of pity.

It is likely, then, that within this family
a dream must be a meeting of the dead and the living.

Pete loves the dreaming ache of me this Christmas. I am the same age
that he last lived.

And Pete must gather that these visits will come nearer
and soon turn altogether into my own
cussed death.

# RAIN WHERE IT DOES NOT BELONG

When I walk out on the ice it is traveling
and when I breathe and blow fog

      I am magnified...

ice-fishing with my dad this is how I measure
what is not straight.

Where we expect snow, rain on its high horse
thaws the ice, erodes with eternal fitness
and goose lands
anticipating open water.  She amplifies.

We gossip about fish.

In my world now is the incense of beast
the drowsy veins of fish set a speck apart.
Finally I am stiff from the cold
and not my joints.

Come inside the cramped ice-shack now:
stoke the heater
drink a little schnaps
smoke
blow your nose
cuss the godforsaken wind that mauls us:

How miserable those brothers of mine
would find the rain. They'd fish for whatever is biting.

A hoop of open water is widening
and turning at the shore. The ice sounds out, creasing
but the center holds
us on the winter lake, a slab of floating chill.

Each hole drilled is rare
a mirror where it does not belong
and we stare into the crystal dark of water to see
the sky
reflected, and rain falling

spiritual and mechanical in the same drop.  Same motion
as ashes to ashes.

No daydream like the thin blue pottery of ice
sealing the hole again, so slowly
each dream is only the size of one fish.
So slowly I've kept a diary
of these dreams since birth.

For dad, the dream is the weight of a fish
and the expectation in his hands. Bare hands
on the ice are the vital signs
of vital signs.  His life is gathered by chewing
but on the ice he slows down that gnawing
and raises himself off the lake
with his lungs.

If I could breathe that large I would travel
the sky, big winter lung
and rise more swiftly than the need for this hunting.

Some fish bite exactly on the heart beat...

Hand over hand
we'll tug to lift a fish through the ice,
and there a cold shedding of lake water drips down its body.
Those drops rinse from a fish, run like bare-faced crying
eased out when a family of brothers
splits its allegiances.

There is no need for both of us to fall through.

He says he'll go now to put down the ladder
to bridge the shore and ice
so we can walk out at dark over the ring of open water.

There goes the composure
of his stocky body shrinking down the horizon.  Next step
he could plunge down, same motion
as a waterfall.  Only a waterfall does not shake its head
asking where his sons are driven to.

Now in his absence my back is to the wind, all that wind.
Like always, instead of that arrow-bone bite of a fish

the next tug running through my arm
could be a gross albatross of bird
finishing its dive

to pluck me off the ice, some impressionable prey
and carry me over to a thicket of tamaracks
to pick me clean.

How magnificient
I dream these faces. Bird. And my dad's...
the last human.

# RHINELANDER

*for Roy Anderson*


How did I ever part from the transistor radio
the open-mouthed coo
of it in the dark?
This night I unpack my goods, having hitched a ride
and opened my palm
around one piece of fruit as it dripped down
three separate truck doors
onto miles of road.
Here I come
to accept the receipt of truth, to align
with the fantasy of a winged worker ant
and to work hard enough that sweat
frozen in my clothes I hang to dry
will arise tomorrow and cool me.
I cough and it is lonely. My slow cigarette
goes out. I budge
like a heavy strap to relight it and breathe
with the glow once more.
Here I come
to hush.

\*\*\*


When I came to the country a meteorite crashed
into the lake. I was familiar
with eclipses and borealis but not this heat.
And not the warm lull whisking
through dead reeds.

\*\*\*


Sun ends in water. I am made fertile by its setting
with fishline in hand, and sometimes a pike
at end—this walleye, turned
from the center of its own face.
Hands around a cider jug follow along
with my gulping mouth, my motions
after I see the age-old fish
fly at the evolving waterbug. Those ghosts of sun

in the shallows breed hard, but water mixed
with pine tannin is the ambush of sun.
What survives when I lift anchor?

\*\*\*


No storm tonight either.
The breeze taps the triangle
of rowboat, a hint of a good rain to come.
I am angered by dry tamarack needles
on the roof of the cabin. If only to run
and shut the windows, and first thing in the morning to bail
the crush of rain in the rowboat. To smell
cedar wood good as my favorite flower.
I'd take the roof off the cabin and heap this shade over the sun, but
I must wet my lips and dream
for tornadoes.
The next day that comes without sun I'll nap at the dock
and sweep the red soot from my eyes.
Stretch, smooth as a sip of water and sleep with everything
white that stands
out before the storm.

\*\*\*


The turtle carries fish eggs from lake to lake in the swamp
of its shell.
Its feet thump the same as a rush of insect wings or fish tails
or hips unbuckled in sex.
I thought I would need to wait until the end of the world
to see this.

\*\*\*


I lose the name I had for the geese. I belong to their day
of most vulnerable migration.
I begin to chew like them.
I push off from the bank. My limbs crouch, mammal-pawed
and I row in this hollow bone. Seated on the bow
my foot in the water
I would be easy for monsters to climb.

\*\*\*

I carry flour, crackers, and beer
splashed on my pants. A batter
recorded there for days.
To eat an animal
we remove its skin. We
take it on that trip.

\*\*\*


Tonight we ask one more time if a fish suffocates.
Here's one secret in our fishing...
one strike
twenty years ago, the canepole I used
at our first creek bent
incongruous
to any strain in water I knew, an aberration
that changed the shock
of hunting for me.
A fish I cannot admit to you that I lost
even now when results
for us are sought
in other loves.

\*\*\*


Hunting frogs for bass bait I am gentle
as the under-chins
of these amphibians.
A hunter has a name with many syllables
but prefers the jargon
of wet nights, accompanied by the fearful dark
in a frog's mouth. The day already captured
in pale undersides
of mimosa ferns, the frog has fed once today
and gone blind
with the reflection on its sticky tongue.
Forward in galoshes I stir up the mirror
of pond, and other
than my hunched figure
I lose the bass notes in the frog's breath.
And this I can only recover
by raining? No, by waiting
which is the true human storm.

\*\*\*

80

My tongue so quiet it rests in a globe
of mouth, a bare whistle efficient as
that redwing blackbird clipping tops of marsh grass
to sew the insect inside her body.
When I learn
my eyes are colored
the green of weeds seen downstream.

\*\*\*

The last I saw tonight was an argeopie
that had built its web under the lamp
and now waited, golden
and hanging, for dark. A culprit
changing his colors for the moths. My thumbs
I do not need, or fingers
for they know grace only
when clenching themselves.
They are not so gentle to know the difference
between a pulse
or a wringing
inside my chest.

\*\*\*

Each poem, not monumental
enough to fill a bird's beak.

\*\*\*

The back of my throat tastes of bleach. Is that dread
of the city? There, light has mass
and is pulled into the strangest...
what is strange is that light does not know history.
Only place. It is a sculptor, shows where
one crack between planks
of the dock widens
while another narrows.

A bumblebee can be in my drinking glass and then
across the bay of this horseshoe lake
in a few seconds. When I am miles away, the worst light
erases the face of the woman I love.
Which is larger, this lake
or that light?

CIRRUS

# HORIZON

*for Greg Klassen and Irma Yepez*


*The Anishinaabeg first told us how our Earth was created. Wenebojo was the first human. With the animals, he shared a place now gone, swept away, that lay where our land of Wisconsin is now. He could talk amongst the animals. His only other company were evil spirits, the manidog. One day he angered them so that they let loose a flood. The waters, under control of the manidog, chased him and stranded him in the tallest pine tree.*

*The flood subsided at a point just below Wenebojo's nose. He saw the animals swimming around his tree, and asked them—one at a time—to dive down and bring up a little earth, so they all might begin again and live on a new land. First the loon tried, then the otter, and the beaver. They all drowned before they resurfaced.*

*The muskrat dove, finally. He passed out as he came to the surface. Wenebojo just about broke down, thinking the feat impossible. Just then, he noticed that the muskrat clutched something in his paw—a few specks of sand and a streak of mud. Maybe it was the hope that came to Wenebojo, because he was able to breath life into the muskrat, and once the animal revived, Wenebojo—still in the pine—looked out to the horizon, rolling the sand and mud in his hands.*

*He soon shaped this little bit of earth into a small island. The animals climbed to dry land to live together on this new world. Wenebojo asked a bird to fly around the island, hoping to expand it as far as the bird could see. The bird flew for nearly a week, but Wenebojo's plan was bigger. He asked the eagle to fly to the horizon and make the land even greater.*

*Wenebojo, done creating the land we know now, called on his family, their families, and so on, to always keep this their home.*

\*\*\*


The horizon for you is turbulence, homage
to this one line of rebirth.

        A horizon
that sustains the divide and meld
of a sky and water, who

evaporate and float
constantly into each other's home.

Wenebojo called on the animals, and you call out to colors...
colors the shade of sand and clay
and mud. Maybe, too, that color of muscles
made for swimming and flying.

Colors, primary
like the sacrifice of the loon.

I wish the animals could come and help you paint...
not to hurry you along, but to save you
for keeping constant watch on the horizon.
In this day and age you have needed to learn to dive
for raw materials
in the same breath as creating the horizon.

Your horizon starts as a scrap or two. Then, the rolling together
of these colors becomes do or die
and you are immersed. Slow progress is made
until one painting is really exercise for the next.

You never perfect any one painting, but you move on
to the next...how is it that a roomful of horizons
can progress all at once?

You need an eagle for that work.

She is in the wind that surrounds you. Flies around your island
made of colors and years
and sees it tip to tip, from where you stand
to the horizon. She expands your work

and sometimes, to do so, flies to places you cannot see or hear
or understand. Then you fear
she will not return, that she has forgotten
or cannot comprehend
all that you want to create. She is, after all, not beside you.
She does not depend on the job to paint
the horizon to sustain her, as you do.

When she comes back, she still smells and feels of the horizon
she traveled to. What is this?

All the while you doubted her heart
she had you in mind. She moved your original horizon
in all directions.

To salvage some hope you had conceded it was better to work
with the horizon alone
for no one could appreciate it the way you do.

So you labored the vision top to bottom
and layer over layer. But she comes back

and one glimpse of her is a glimpse in the same moment
of the original idea
and the wider, finished picture. It seems possible
that all the tinkering mechanics of painting are present

only to keep you busy, to hold you on Earth
when surely the awe of trusting her
the way you do
would turn you into the exhilarated stuff of clouds
she travels through.

Will you ever know what the horizon means
to her? She does not live for it, she approached it
when you asked, and even if you had not asked
she would encounter the horizon daily
without effort

simply because she is the eagle

you chose when you needed someone in the same motion
to sacrifice
and survive.

# IMMIGRANT WEDDING SONG

All immigrants owning even half an imagination
saw ivory flashes of bombs take down landmarks
that night in the city...

and considered
how the story of how they met and married—that passion—
would survive in the hands of their families...
and children waiting to be born.

How we met and married, that story needed proof...

love letters
wedding pictures
affidavits

so in her eyes this ivory light became bombs: it reflected

off hot mirrors
in a copy machine atop the library
and flashed on windows
facing the view of downtown

and the white glare, transposed
on glass, appeared as bombs
exploding on banks and hotels.

Our marriage certificate blasted the last shred of neon downtown...
the Wisconsin Gas building, its red or blue flame
to predict sun or storm, or flashing yellow for a change
in the weather...gone now
to prove our marriage genuine.

        All materials copied to apply for citizenship
became the stuff of bombs...
birth certificates
vaccination records
and X-rays.

Was it the questions on government forms, marked with fear
that tempted our imagination?

Are you a member of the Communist party?
A sexual deviant?

Now in the making of this disaster, the city
spilled into its own wounds.
These ivory flashes...was America taking
some of its own medicine?

How we met and married...how will she become American
if our story does not survive? The anthem
is supposed to give us proof through this night.
Bombs are part of the song.

Is it the fear in these questions that tempts us to lie
when there is no cause...that will make us change
our story until it is lost?

Tonight we are tired of all the places we can scatter to
in this big world, and all without common, blood-related shelter.

What to do with these strange ideas of my family in America
seeking more proof day and night?
The folks, where will they end up
when they finish tearing up their own manual for marriage?

One brother, catching himself: "I'd be a rich—I mean, a richer—man, if..."

The other, I remember him fit for a parade
done up in his military outfit, dressed gray
over gray, the outdated saber hung on hip.

                    The act of a sword
is to draw a line in the dirt, daring the enemy to cross. What challenges
he could shout tonight with that tough, apple-core of a mouth.

If only he had sent just a card for our wedding.
Maybe he needed more proof
that our match would last.

                Some sent instructions
with money to buy ourselves a little something
and the rest, factory seconds.

Those gifts are bombed tonight out of the cupboards
and closets, accustomed to jumping down
and crashing when we fight for our wedding song.

Doubts in those gifts can wear the proof thin.

Now, with the white fire in our own hands, we call on the oldest

of immigrants. Used to be, they feared
falling off the edge of the sea when traveling to the New World.

Likewise, the new monsters are ivory bombs, imagined by fear of ungodly
arrogance in America, and the revenge
coming closer from inside and out...

All my life I've wanted a foreign wife. Early on the "want"
was ugly song—I did not know the evil in wishing
for pure blood. Grandpa's looks
I wanted.

       I was not careful
and made wishes that can take me from my home

                         for not in my country
will my wife bring a child into the world.
Too many dangers come when one is born
an American...
dangers longer than a parent's arms.

And when I agree, how will those first immigrants in the family
respond, dead adrift now in clouds
after their worse journey to Wisconsin?

Am I their "If I could do it all over again..."
or do I abandon their spirits sifting in clouds
still working to make Wisconsin home?

This story I tell on the road out of town...
is all the proof they need of how we met and continue
to be married.

    Let fall their gifts.

# MANŽELKA

My wife

will call out to our child with the right accent, for its name
will not be American.

I would need to travel back in time to pronounce it
just so

but the language the child knows from birth
in the Old Country
will shape its jaw

               and the countenance of those ancestors
in the clouds will come alive.

Great-Grandpa Krist...his first wife, before Katerína, died in childbirth
with the baby. I'm sure he would have chosen to die instead.
Instead, he set out for America.

Day by day he watched his wife
become a mother.
Then, he abandons home. How not to?

Somewhere in Milwaukee lies a rotten hull of a ship
where my great-grandpa forced hope
on himself, then struggled up to the island
that is America.

My wife asks me to feel the baby inside
and to listen. Sometimes, when her belly is quiet, I think
both have died.
That they will go on expecting right into the dark.

                              Then a beautiful rain of hiccup
and heartbeat comes and I know a new home is ahead.

Krist, I got a family coming now, and we are going
against wishes.

What was your baby's name to be? You brought danger
to your wife. We all do. Babies come out
one way or another, we know that one thing.

                    Even now we are warned
about ways our baby could die. Reminded

of how bad people
have it outside America.

They have in mind, Krist, us godforsaken immigrants.

# CONVECTION

I wait for you to lie on your back beside me, a little turtle
eager to tell me what shapes you glimpse in the clouds.

The buoyancy of these clouds moves us to tears.

Fall asleep under the clouds
and your dreams will be made of smooth wood.
Rain does nice things to wood.

Clouds are boats of momentum
rising from striking storm to feather ice. Evolving shapes of just one cloud
show us potential
that an island-full of people cannot muster.

Ancestors are clouds. All neighbors and strangers
we'll ever see, and prior generations
jostle in layers and eras of clouds. Their revolutions and happy feasts
accompany:

Ice age clouds
Indian clouds
French missionary clouds
Declaration of Independence clouds
Black Hawk War clouds
Immigrant clouds
Sawmill, factory, and farm clouds
Brewery clouds
Socialist clouds
World War clouds
Braves Win the Pennant! clouds
Ginsberg exorcising McCarthy's grave clouds
Walleye Warrior clouds

The dead are clouds
and the dead bring rain.

Every breath of all who called Wisconsin home
is recycled in the clouds.

Girl or boy
tell stories about what you find when you glimpse the clouds...

shapes cordate or lenticular:

a pregnant ladybug
          sustaining our wishes

footprints made for history
          in the fresh sidewalk

a little one reaching for the moon
          undressing for the bath

a fish under a tree
          whispering your name.

You are soon due and as I wait I am finding
your mouth and eyes...

but what cloud is not an ear? Your whole body

learns its shape leaning gratefully on the inside
of your mother, the only boundary
you know until born.

After, boundaries do strange things
to the spirit. Add to that the give-and-take pressure
of all that arranges in the clouds.

Already I talk
you into a name, auditioning it somehow

also, I
talk like steam gathering
not on something fixed, but on more of the same
conjectures. Maybe that's my job...

I'll teach you how to talk. There you will take my advice.

Yet, so much we hear
is not what is
told to us.

And what we know the world does to us
is gained by looking at a father's face

when he's half-ashamed
                and the other half is rushing to get to work.

## DIET'A

Krist and Katarína, in your *Výskonsan* clouds
you know by now that we are expecting
a little dievča or chlapec.

Is this enough to swing you up from nimbus storms
toward cirrus, and your shapes tear to feathers?

Do you know, is the baby mužske or ženské?

We'll not ruin that surprise
using machines. What is an ultrasound

but noise sent over the range of our hearing...and what better
than your voices raining from the clouds?

        Now we move alphabetically, listening for names
in the family. Soon, time will come to speak to the dieťa
po slovensky.

        English formed with an open scar on my tongue.

This is my oldest story.

I was just learning to talk.
Fell off a kitchen counter, in a split-second my jaw hit the edge.
Maybe in that time I jabbered the few *exact* words I would ever know.

So when my teeth clamped down I only let go a trickle of blood from my tongue.
Did not 'open up' for three days, and ate nothing.
No talking. Drank the blood
and infection, until the doctor told us
I bit through all but a sliver of my tongue.

I started to speak again, manipulating this lousy mouth. Every letter
was a meticulous failure, each story I told
a test
to choose the right word to avoid the pain. "S" sounds serrated.
Any story with an "S" I'd hiss, stop, and unsure...
drink the noise back in.

In this strange library I still make my noise. Learning to speak slovenčina
makes the scar stand out.

My own name, should it be pronounced right
I would not stumble: Tomašovič...

'sh' instead of 's', and not 'Too-mas-a-vich,' the way my folks
would sound it out, the reception desk too high for me
to see the nurse. Too difficult a name

but by now, not difficult enough. Malleable. American, all the same.


                                        Your birth
certificates, no one at the reunion this summer could read.

Was that enough to propel you out of the low nimbus
toward a scant, and more distant memory in high cirrus?

Not even Joe, the eldest son, could decipher the sparse forms
prepared in Communist Československa. The family needed an inkling of Slovak yet

to know your history was transferred
from elaborate pages of a birth book in your hometown...Igram, a village
in the old Austria-Hungary Empire.

"Kristian" and "Katarína", handwritten.
Recorded in volumes of vellum and dyes, these books
dedicated to match the magic handiwork of birth.

Relayed later, using stock courier, in the central Bratislava office.
The vellum pages too big, too fragile for a copy machine.

Again, the official forms confirmed that the Old Country was a stark place
not accustomed to celebrating, and fit only for escape. No wonder
Jozef and Mária named you Krist, Great-Grandpa.

Katarína, the duplicates were your doing, no? To complete the application
for American citizenship. All you wanted was the privilege
to vote for a prezidentovi.

                Two years in the first grade for Joe, to learn English
in the Thornapple school to become a little Američan.
Come reunion time, his Slovak evaporated.

Dear Joe,

Your daughter, Rose, I believe has told you about me...I am your great-nephew,
Bryan Tomasovich, grandson of your brother Frank, and youngest son of Frank
Jr. (or Sonny). Perhaps we met when I was a little boy. I am glad to write you
this letter...

...Did your parents ever speak about the spelling of our last name, or perhaps
indicate why they changed the spelling of it from  Tomašovič to Tomasovich
(you probably know the Slovak "š" is pronounced like the English "sh", and "č"
like "ch"—and we pronounce our name close-to-correctly although the spelling
is changed—unlike those relatives who go by Tomasovic now, with the hard "k"
at the end).

...in closing, one thing I should tell you that I am up to is learning Slovak. A
young Slovak man teaches me. I met him when I joined a society of Czech and
Slovak artists and scientists now living in America. He introduced himself,
speaking Slovak—"but your jaw, and forehead," he said, when I apologized for
not speaking one word. Strange, as I announced that I am American I did not
look him in the eye, but around the room—with a shake of the imagination, the
gathering turned into a family reunion. I'll keep working at the language, for I
believe it is 'a must' if we want to recover some of the Slovak culture that is lost
in our families. As far as I know, in our family the language lives on through
you only.

Perhaps I can make the Tomasovich reunion this summer, and see you then. Na
skoro.

D`akujem, a do videnia.


            Krist and Katarína, I missed the reunion.

Only one-half of your lives was legible for the family.
Your naturalization certificates
gave proof of a second birth
full of stories, so comprehensible...

Kristian is white with a "dark complexion," and Katarína fair
with a mole on her face, excited about the election.

Both appear in grayscale in copies mailed to me after the reunion.
Out of the envelope, upside-down
came Katarína's Certificate of Naturalization

and widow's peak, tussled hair, nose, chin, half-frown, you name it...
I am the spitting image of her
photo, upside-down and once blurred by machine.

          Now the child readies itself, turning upside-down for delivery
to my hands.

We prepare for a homebirth. But, Krist and Katarína, kde je domov...
where is home? Výskonsan?

No matter its likeness to me, our dieťa comes with a perfect tongue.
Where must we go, so a 'homebirth' is not a lie
we are preparing for the child?

# LOOK INSIDE CLOUDS

Clouds, immigrate.
Closer, blow storm
blow imbroglio
bring fresh stories in new wind to our neighborhood.

Flinch the horsehair measuring humidity
in the museum. Clouds, prove
that someone walks beside us.
Shadow, also, the tissue
of our errors.

Sit here on our own dung heap.
New wind

that enters our houses
wave and mix with dreams of tornadoes
and rising water

they are all the love we have

while now we feel all seasons in our dressing
and undressing.

Evaporation in the sky
always a factory of clouds

bring rain.

Let us swear and curse more
the constant Earth we make. Drum down

the wires and poles
and meld the rays to their own satellites.

Blow us seeds and soak
our twigs, change the message of suicide

to a glimpse at your billowing dead.

Do this for friends

and for strangers.

Change our fundamental stones
to anvils of cumulonimbus.

Ice landing in air, change
the changing of the light
in Výskonsan. Clouds

scribble wise rain over my homecoming scribal
or I must emigrate
back to the Old Country.

Look inside us, clouds.
Pour more inside.

# BIBLIOGRAPHY

Anderson, Harry and Frederick Olson. *Milwaukee: At the Gathering of the Waters.* Tulsa, OK: Continental Heritage, 1981.

Bieder, Robert. *Native American Communities in Wisconsin, 1600-1960: A Study of Tradition and Change.* Madison, WI: U. of Wisconsin, 1995.

Bodnar, John. *Remaking America: Public Memory, Commemoration, and Patriotism in the Twentieth Century.* Princeton: Princeton U., 1992.

Bourgeois, Arthur, ed. *Ojibwa Narratives of Charles and Charlotte Kawbawgam and Jacques LePique, 1893-1895.* Detroit: Wayne State U., 1994.

Carlson, Leonard. *Indians, Bureaucrats, and Land: The Dawes Act and the Decline of Indian Farming.* Westport, CT: Greenwood, 1981.

Cronon, William. *Changes in the Land: Indians, Colonists, and the Ecology of New England.* New York: Hill and Wang-FS&G, 1983.

Edmunds, David. *Potawatomis, Keepers of the Fire.* Norman, OK: U. Oklahoma, 1978.

Hickerson, Harold. *The Chippewa and their Neighbors: A Study in Ethnohistory.* New York: Holt, Rinehart and Winston, 1970.

Horsman, Reginald. *Race and Manifest Destiny: The Origins of American Racial Anglo-Saxonism.* Cambridge, MA: Harvard U., 1981.

Johnston, Basil. *Ojibway Heritage.* Lincoln, NE: Nebraska U., 1976.

Korman, Gerd. *Industrialization, Immigrants, and Americanizers: The View from Milwaukee, 1866-1921.* Madison, WI: The State Historical Society of Wisconsin, 1967.

Lapham, Increase. *The Antiquities of Wisconsin.* 1842. New York: AMS, 1973.

---. *Wisconsin: Its Geography and Topography, History, Geology, and Mineralogy, Together with Brief Sketches of its Antiquities, Natural History, Soil, Productions, Population, and Government.* Milwaukee: I.A. Hopkins, 1846.

Meteorological Office. *Cloud Types for Observers.* London: Her Majesty's Stationery Office, 1982.

Meyer, Melissa. *The White Earth Tragedy: Ethnicity and Dispossession at a Minnesota Anishinaabe Reservation, 1889-1920.* Lincoln, NE: Nebraska U., 1994.

Ritzenthaler, Robert. *Prehistoric Indians of Wisconsin.* Milwaukee: Milwaukee Public Museum, 1953.

Vogel, Virgil. *American Indian Medicine.* Norman, OK: U. Oklahoma, 1970.

White, Richard. *The Middle Ground: Indians, Empires, and Republics in the Great Lakes Region, 1650-1815.* Cambridge, UK: Cambridge U., 1991.

BRYAN TOMASOVICH is the winner of the Emergency Press annual book contest for 2003. He grew up in Wisconsin and now lives on Bainbridge Island, Washington. Tomasovich teaches at Antioch University Seattle, where he is the faculty editor of KNOCK.

Author portrait by André Pretorius

*Ouisconsin: The Dead in Our Clouds* was designed by Jason Gitlin with help from Jennifer Furman and Laurentiu Ardelean.

Printed in the U.S.A. by Lightning Source on acid-free, 30% post-consumer content recycled paper.

Emergency Press participates in the Green Press Initiative, a non-profit organization that is, "working to advance the inclusion of environmental and social impacts as additional measures of corporate success. These ecological goals for industry transformation include:

- Responsible Fiber Sourcing in Paper Production through the elimination of book papers with fiber that originates from endangered forests

- Maximizing the Use of Postconsumer Recycled and Alternative Fibers as a means of supporting the continued development of an environmentally superior fiber infrastructure

- Minimizing Consumption as the most effective means of conserving resources.

- Preferencing Chlorine Free Products in an effort to support bleaching processes that minimize toxic discharges in our waterways"

Emergency Press is the imprint of the Emergency Collective. A New York non-profit organization, the press is also a member and grant recipient of The Council of Literary Magazines and Presses, and a participant in the Green Press Initiative. The collective also publishes an on-line, bi-annual magazine, *The Emergency Almanac.*

The Emergency Collective is a group of writers that united in 2001 to bridge what we consider artificial and counterproductive divides in contemporary literature. We don't see significant distinctions between high art and journalism, accessibility and sophistication, physical and metaphysical, or form and content.

Instead, we try to highlight the social relevance of our inquiries through the fusion of such divides. One way we do this is through the hands-on investigation of issues that are on the verge of emerging from the unconscious commonplace into collective emergencies.

We also apply our vision through our democratic publishing practices, by which every member helps to direct the output of the collective, through either collaboration, editing one another's work, judging for the annual Emergency Press book contest, or even by sending other *Emergency Almanac* reporters 'on assignment'.

Emergency Press
531 W. 25th St.
New York, NY 10001
emergencypress.org
press@emergencypress.org

\*\*\*

Emergency Press will donate 10% from the sales of *Ouisconsin: The Dead in Our Clouds* to the American Civil Liberties Union Foundation. This contribution is part of a larger initiative at Emergency Press to give a portion of our sales to progressive organizations that align with the central theme of each book we publish.

In as much as *Ouisconsin: The Dead in Our Clouds* reports on immigration, we wish to promote the work carried out by the ACLU's Immigrants' Rights Project.

An on-line study guide, or 'primer', meant to complement *Ouisconsin: The Dead in Our Clouds* is available on the Emergency Press web site: emergencypress.org

Printed in the United States
40486LVS00007B/280

9 780975 362303